I0104195

Why would I want to

HIRE A
DIVORCE
LAWYER

anyway?

A guide to hiring an attorney
(or not) – for women only.

By Katie Wilcox Carter, Esq.

*Why would I want to **hire a divorce lawyer**, anyway?*

Copyright ©2025 by Hofheimer Family Law Firm

All Rights Reserved. No part of this book may be used or reproduced in any manner whatsoever without written permission of the author.

Printed in the United States of America.

ISBN: 979-8-218-62012-7

Hofheimer Family Law Firm
1604 Hilltop West Executive Center, Suite 300
Virginia Beach, VA 23451
HofLaw.com

TABLE OF CONTENTS

Introduction   4

Chapter 1: Do I even need a lawyer?   9

Chapter 2: I need to hire a family law attorney.   31

Chapter 3: Finding a Family Law Attorney   50

Chapter 4: Choosing a Family Law Attorney   67

Attorney / Firm Evaluation Form   105

Conclusion   108

Disclaimer: *This book is based upon Virginia law. While the various jurisdictions have similar laws and processes related to divorce and child custody, the reader will find this book helpful for informational purposes. This book gives general information based upon Virginia family law and is not intended to be used as specific legal advice. Please consult with an attorney licensed in your jurisdiction with significant experience in family law for specific legal advice regarding your family law case.*

Introduction

Hi! My name is Katie Wilcox Carter, and I've worked as a Virginia family law attorney dedicated to representing women exclusively in divorce, custody, and support for over a decade.

I get a lot of questions all the time about the divorce and custody process, including hiring an attorney – or not. Though the actual ins and outs of custody cases is a bit beyond the scope of this book, I do recommend that you check out *What Every Virginia Woman Needs to Know About Divorce,* the *Women's Custody Survival Guide, the Virginia Military Wives Guide to Divorce,* as well as our two seminars, *What Every Virginia Woman Needs to Know About Divorce,* and *Custody Bootcamp for Moms.*

In this book, I'm here to discuss two important questions: first, do I need a Virginia family law attorney, and, secondly, if I DO need an attorney in my upcoming divorce or custody case – then who?

I'm under no illusions. You've probably picked up this book hoping to find out that you don't need an attorney after all.

You probably haven't even come into contact with that many attorneys throughout your life. Sure, if you purchased a house, there was a real estate attorney.

If you're extremely proactive, you may have met with a wills and estates lawyer. If you're unlucky, maybe a criminal or traffic lawyer. It's possible, too, if you've been in an accident that you will have met a personal injury attorney. But none of these things are everyday occurrences. At least, not for most people.

Family law attorneys are different in a lot of ways from the other kinds of lawyers that you may (or, probably more likely, may not) have had experience with up to this point in your life. Family law cases, too, are different from a lot of other types of cases, mostly in the sense that the impact that a divorce or custody case can have on your life will most likely be profound.

Not only do divorce and custody cases handle custody and visitation of minor children (which is often one of the most contentious points of any family law case), but we handle all the details that make up the rest of your life too – from child and spousal support, to how to divide retirement, investment, and bank accounts, to whether you'll keep or sell the house, and more. Family law touches your day to day life in a way that a lot of other types of law don't.

A family law attorney is someone who helps handle some of the most intimate decisions of your life; the attorney you hire should be someone who you can trust implicitly.

For that reason, it's extra important to hire an attorney – if you decide to hire an attorney – with whom you can be honest. In family law, we regularly have to talk to our clients about things that are a little uncomfortable – finances, sex, parenting, and the health of their marriage. Though I think very few clients go into the attorney/client relationship intending to be dishonest, a lot of factors (like, embarrassment or shame) can cause a client to tell a fib or stretch a truth.

I get it! A lot of times, we have to give clients advice that they don't want to hear. It can be really scary to find out that something that you've taken for granted – like, maybe, that moms always win custody – isn't true. It can be even more jarring to hear your attorney describe what a reasonable result in your case might look like. If you get specific advice that you don't want to hear – like that you should probably not be living with your current boyfriend, given his criminal background, or that you absolutely cannot just relocate to Michigan, where your family all lives – it's tempting to plug your ears and hum.

"But I thought your firm were advocates for women!"

We – me, and the other attorneys at the Virginia based family law firm where I've worked for the past decade (and then some) – are definitely advocates for women! But that doesn't mean that we can always tell every specific woman exactly what she wants to hear. Not giving you the answer you want, though, doesn't mean that your attorney – if you chose to hire someone from our office – isn't advocating for your best interests.

In fact, I'd venture to say, whether you hire someone from our office or somewhere else in Virginia, you're likely to receive advice, at some point, that you don't really like. Hearing something that you don't like, or something that doesn't quite tally with what you understand about how the law works in Virginia, can quickly erode the relationship between an attorney and a client, if you've hired someone that you don't feel you can completely trust.

It's a big deal to hire an attorney, especially in a divorce and custody case. There's a lot at stake. In a lot of ways, your life is probably about to completely change. Some of those changes will be good – great, even – and some of those, well, probably less so.

It's stressful, overwhelming, and you're probably full of a million different feelings – sadness, regret, anger, resentment, fear – and, even, maybe, cautious happiness, hope, and relief. Ending your marriage is a big decision. So, too, is hiring an attorney – or deciding, perhaps, NOT to hire an attorney.

Let me help take one thing off your plate.

The only person who should decide whether to hire an attorney – and if so, whom – is you. But you might not have all the information at your disposal that you might want to have when faced with such an important (and potentially life altering choice). I can help you there.

Chapter 1

Do I even need a lawyer?

I know, I know. You're not-so-secretly hoping you can do this without hiring a lawyer. It's totally normal.

You're probably also thinking, "You're a lawyer; why would you tell me that I can do this without one?" After all, representing women in family law cases is how I make a living!

It may sound self-serving, but the reality is that it is actually very, very difficult to manage a custody, visitation, child support, spousal support, or divorce case on your own.

When someone represents themselves in court, we call them a 'pro se' litigant. 'Pro se' means 'on one's own behalf' in Latin. It's important, because it describes the way the court looks at this class of people. They're not in court WITHOUT an attorney; they're acting as an attorney themselves.

This is an important distinction. You're not someone who doesn't have an attorney; you're acting as your attorney yourself. It's probably safe to say that you're not held to quite the standard that a licensed, barred attorney would be, but you are still expected to know the law and the local rules of the court in which you are appearing, which is no small task.

There aren't a lot of resources for pro se litigants, and there are certainly no step-by-step how-to guides. There are law libraries (most law schools and many courtrooms have them) and the internet, but you'll have to do a lot of digging, in general, to get the information you need to successfully move your case forward without a lawyer.

You probably know that already, though, right? That's what lawyers do, too. It's not like we just show up in court at the appointed hour and dazzle the judge and jury. (By the way, maybe a good time to mention that there are no juries in family law cases in Virginia.) There's a lot to know. The law changes, sometimes more than once a year. It varies dramatically from state to state; Virginia is absolutely not the same as North Carolina or Maryland.

Not only that, but courts also have their own rules that you must know and follow.

Obviously, it's easier to represent yourself in easier cases than difficult ones. In general, I would not recommend representing yourself in a difficult case where litigation is involved, with one possible exception. Let's talk through some of the common scenarios that I see where it might be possible to represent yourself.

Where you want a divorce and it's 'amicable' because no one wants anything from anybody.

It's easy, right? No one wants anything from anyone. Maybe it was even a super short marriage, so there's not much to divide anyway.

The problem is that, in Virginia, you need to either get a separation agreement in place or litigate how everything in your case will be divided. Either way, it needs to be fairly comprehensive. It's not as simple as saying "We don't want anything from each other." You need to list each and every asset, liability, or responsibility that you've accumulated between you during the marriage and specify exactly what will happen to it moving forward.

Even for otherwise separate property – property to which you or he would have no legal entitlement – it's a good idea to explicitly name it and specify the party to whom it belongs.

A separation agreement – basically a legal contract that specifically divides all the assets, liabilities, and responsibilities formally between parties to a divorce action – is a complicated document full of places where major (read: expensive) mistakes can be made.

Are you sure you want nothing from him? Are you aware of the extent of your specific entitlements? Do you have children in common? If so, certainly custody, visitation, and child support will need to be determined, and, frankly, that's often a minefield of potential problems.

You may find, after you dig into the assets, liabilities, and responsibilities, that it's not really as simple as you were expecting. Drafting the agreement, too, can be challenging. And even once you've drafted an agreement, you'll still have to go through the uncontested divorce process.

Theoretically, it is possible to represent yourself. But that doesn't mean it's easy, and it doesn't mean that you won't make mistakes.

I do have some recommendations for how you should proceed, if you're still interested – but stick with me as I discuss one more category first.

Where you have a separation agreement already and it's just a matter of obtaining an uncontested divorce.

Whether you've done it yourself (be careful!) or have worked with an attorney or mediator, you may already have a separation agreement in place.

After the separation agreement is finalized and you've both signed (ideally, in front of a notary – though that's not legally required), you're not divorced. You still have to go through the uncontested divorce process, which mostly involves paperwork.

Each court is a little bit different, so you should familiarize yourself with your local court's procedures. In some courts, you're required to attend an in-person uncontested divorce hearing if you lived separate and apart under the same roof for any period of your one year (or six months, if you have no minor children and the agreement already signed) separation. Many do not require an in person hearing and you're able to complete a divorce by affidavit only.

It's a matter of filling out the right paperwork – filing a complaint, if you haven't already, having it served on your partner (or being served yourself), the respondent filing (or at least having had an opportunity, in the form of 21 elapsed days, to have done so) a responsive pleading, and then a prepared uncontested divorce packet, including, but not limited to, the final decree of divorce, any QDROs (if you need one of these, you really should talk to an attorney), VS4, confidential addendum, name change order, and so on.

Does it sound like a lot? Well, frankly, it kind of is! It's not that it's hard so much as it's a lot of different moving pieces, and you have to make sure all the pieces are there, are consistent, and take care of what needs to be resolved. A name change after your divorce is finalized, for example, is more difficult. A QDRO (qualified domestic relations order) dividing your tax deferred retirement assets between the two of you really needs to be handled contemporaneously, or you risk all sorts of things happening to that money before you get your share.

In other words, the more time passes, the harder it can be to get what you are entitled to receive. It may even become impossible. It doesn't mean that you can't do it, but it is something that you should be aware of before you attempt it.

I still want to attempt to represent myself. What should I do? Where should I start?

Sure! I get it – a lot of people would prefer to navigate their cases without hiring a lawyer. If you're determined, and willing to put the work in, it's not impossible!

Request a free copy of our divorce book for Virginia women.

You'll want to educate yourself first. We offer several free books (like this one!) – one for regular divorce, one for military divorce (if you're military or former military, you don't need both – just the military book), and a third for custody and visitation.

I definitely recommend you check them out as a starting point. It's not a complete primer on how to handle your case yourself, but the books – especially taken together with custody and visitation – are a great way to learn about the divorce and custody case process in Virginia.

Learn more: https://hoflaw.com/resources/

Attend a monthly divorce seminar.

In conjunction with our books, we also offer a monthly divorce seminar. Each seminar is taught live on

Zoom by one of our licensed and experienced Virginia divorce and custody attorneys.

Notably, the seminar includes the opportunity for Q&A with the attorney. Because it's not a confidential forum (there are, after all, other attendees), we ask that you keep the questions fairly general, rather than case-specific, and we can't review documents, but, otherwise, questions are fair game.

It's a great opportunity to ask those can't-eat-can't-sleep questions that keep you lying awake at night.

Check out what other resources are available.

While I don't know of a comprehensive service that will help you handle your own divorce, there are some resources out there. I do always caution people who are looking online for resources to make sure that whatever they're reading is up to date, Virginia specific, and created by actual, practicing lawyers. It's very easy to fall into a trap online where you don't know where information has come from. While that's fine for some things, you'll want to make sure that it's all accurate as far as your Virginia divorce and/or custody case is concerned. There's a lot at stake!

The Virginia State Bar has a 'self help' program, as well as some informational brochures, available for pro se litigants.

Virginia Legal Aid also has an uncontested divorce worksheet with instructions, and it's sponsored by the Virginia Poverty Law Center.

The Norfolk Circuit Court has a pro se uncontested divorce manual as well.

Please make sure you get your information from a reputable source!

No matter what, do it yourself divorce is a big commitment – and you'll need to make sure that you're willing to put in the time and effort to do it properly. Or don't, but the only two people who'll pay the consequences are you and your soon-to-be ex.

What about custody and visitation cases?

Many times, custody and visitation are part of an underlying divorce case, and those cases are handled in circuit court.

Sometimes, though, that's not the case – whether because you and your child's father never married, or because you're already divorce and are modifying an existing custody and visitation agreement or court order.

In those cases, custody, visitation, and/or child support will be determined in juvenile court.

In general, we do not recommend representing yourself in a contested case, whether we're talking about custody and visitation or divorce. There is one exception, though, where it may be possible to represent yourself – and this is it.

When custody, visitation, and/or child support are determined in juvenile court, it's automatically appealable to the circuit court.

Don't get it wrong, though. When you go through the juvenile court, a Guardian ad litem may be appointed (which you may be responsible for paying for). If you can't reach an agreement, you will have a trial, with witnesses, exhibits, and evidence, in front of a judge, who will render a decision. That judge's order will stand until your appeal (if you timely file an appeal) is heard in front of the circuit court judge. At that point, you could win or you could lose a second time.

In general, juvenile court is considered to be more user friendly than circuit court. Additionally, the fact that you can get an automatic appeal to circuit court – an appeal 'de novo,' which means that you get to have it heard in the circuit court like it's the first time, without anything coming up from the juvenile court – is appealing to many people who'd prefer to represent themselves in their own cases.

At that point, you have two options. First, you could represent yourself in the juvenile court, and then hire an attorney to handle your appeal in circuit court.

Second, custody and visitation are always modifiable based on a material change in circumstances. So, if you don't get a result you like in juvenile court, you appeal to the circuit court and you lose, you can file again, six months to a year later, if your circumstances have changed, and ask again that custody and visitation be modified. You can represent yourself, again, or you could hire an attorney.

You can do this again and again, ad nauseam, until your child turns 18 and the court no longer has authority over custody and visitation. (Likewise – your child's father can take you back to court, over and over, to determine and modify custody and visitation until your child turns 18 and the court no longer has jurisdiction over custody and visitation.)

You can go back to court later – but key players in your case (like judges and Guardians ad litem) will likely follow you.

You can modify an existing custody order or agreement when the 'best interests of the child' warrants it after a 'material change in circumstances'.

But that doesn't mean that you get a brand new do-over. No, actually – far from it. In many cases, the judges you've seen before will hear your case again and any Guardian ad litem who may have been appointed in your previous case will be re-appointed for the modification.

This isn't to punish you; it's to preserve the court's resources and keep familiar parties associated with familiar matters (rather than going to the time and expense of bringing a new person up to speed). Of course, judges and Guardians ad litem do sometimes retire, relocate, and go on maternity leave, so it's always possible that you won't see their familiar faces again. But you definitely should not count on that. You should count on seeing them again, and keep in mind that the impression you make now is very, very important, whether you win or lose.

Whether your case is in juvenile court or circuit court, though, you'd have a trial if you didn't reach an agreement.

When I say that the juvenile court is 'more' user friendly than circuit court, I don't mean to suggest that what you're proposing is easy. Whether you're in juvenile court or circuit court, there are rules that you must follow. You are expected to know these rules.

There are deadlines that apply. You are expected to adhere to these deadlines.

It's not as simple as me listing the rules and/or deadlines here; these can vary dramatically from court to court, with each court following the laws (including case law) of the Commonwealth of Virginia, as well as local rules created and enforced by the locality.

Not only that, but you'll be expected to present evidence, question and cross examine witnesses, and make opening and closing statements.

It's worth mentioning, too, that doing this – remaining calm and cool enough to, say, question a witness in a contested custody trial – is exponentially more difficult when you're emotionally involved because the children who are the subject of the trial are your own.

I want to represent myself. What should I do? Where should I start?

Sure. Lots of people choose to represent themselves, or just try it themselves at first before they ultimately decide to hire an attorney. The hard thing about custody and visitation is that it can be litigated over and over and over again, and it's not ever really over until the child turns 18 and isn't a child anymore, at which point the juvenile court no longer has authority to determine custody and visitation.

In the most acrimonious cases, custody and visitation can be modified over and over which, over time, can amount to a lot in attorney's fees. It's always going to be really difficult to represent yourself in a case with complicated issues, including (but definitely not limited to) physical or sexual abuse, parental alienation, relocation, mental health, and addiction.

Still, there are some resources out there designed to help – but, again, you'll want to make sure that any sources you consult are up to date, Virginia specific, and actually written or created by licensed, experienced, practicing Virginia divorce and custody attorneys.

Download our custody book for Virginia moms

Learning about what a 'material change in circumstances' is or what constitutes the 'best interests of the child' is beyond the scope of this book. But we DO have a book that answers both of those questions – and a whole lot more.

We also have several free reports, on everything from working with a GAL, to how to navigate complex cases, like relocation, reunification, and physical or sexual abuse.

It's always important to understand the law and how it works in Virginia cases!

Attend Custody Bootcamp for Moms

Custody Bootcamp for Moms is an intense, all day seminar designed to teach Virginia moms what they need to know to represent themselves in their juvenile court custody cases. Each seminar is taught by one of our licensed and experienced attorneys and also includes video and other interactive content featuring each of our other attorneys.

But can I really do it without hiring an attorney? Is it worth the risk?

No one else can answer that question for you. In any family law case, there is a lot at stake. Mistakes and omissions can be very costly.

Whenever I meet with a doctor or other professional, I ask them what they would do if they were in my shoes. Would I – if I were you, and not me – represent myself in a divorce or custody case? The answer, for me, is absolutely, positively no.

I usually say that, the way I look at it, I have two jobs: (1) to get you divorced today, and (2) to minimize future problems later on down the line. The divorce itself is only half of the job. A badly written agreement, or a court order that misses a valuable asset, is costly to revisit later on down the line. In my practice, I've seen lots of cases come back with issues from their initial divorce that a knowledgeable, experienced attorney would have caught – thereby saving them thousands or even tens of thousands of dollars.

Would that happen to you? It's hard to say. But I do think that it's very, very clear that a well drafted agreement can prevent a lot of issues from coming up later. (Even with custody and visitation, where it's modifiable based on a material change regardless of how well the agreement is drafted, a good agreement can prevent problems from turning into full blown issues that require additional litigation.)

Can you emotionally handle the stress of representing yourself?

There are a lot of considerations when it comes to whether you'll really be able to represent yourself, and one of the things that you really must consider is whether you have the emotional capacity to handle a lengthy, stressful divorce or custody case on your own.

It is certainly a matter of knowing the law, the court, and the relevant policies and procedures, but it's extra difficult to handle your own case. In fact, attorneys have a saying about this. "An attorney who represents himself has a fool for a client."

I don't mean to suggest that I think that you're a fool if you're considering this. I'm sure that, like almost all of our clients and prospective clients, you're scared and overwhelmed and you're just trying to make the best possible decision in what seems like an impossible situation.

There's no question, though, that dealing with your own case is more emotionally harrowing than dealing with someone else's. Though, as attorneys, we keenly feel the responsibility associated with representing our clients in some of the more challenging moments of our lives, we also aren't personally impacted.

We're not angry. We don't feel personally wronged. We're not fearful for the future. So many of the emotions that you're feeling so viscerally are things that – though we're aware of them – are not clouding our judgment or spurring us to ill-advised action. It's not to say that you can't do it, but that, if you do choose to, it's going to be exponentially more difficult for you to do so, and not just because you don't have the professional experience that a practicing attorney would have.

It's wise to consider your emotional state and whether you're really equipped to handle something of this magnitude before you undertake your own representation. It's also probably going to be especially critical to enlist the support of a mental health professional if you do decide to go down this road so that you can deal with your feelings in as healthy a manner as possible.

Are there alternatives to hiring an attorney?

There are alternatives to hiring an attorney that you may also want to consider, too. One of the most common alternatives is mediation.

Mediation

Mediation can be great, but it can also be a tricky process. A mediator is a person who may or may not be an attorney but, in any case, it doesn't really matter – because it's not the mediator's job to tell you what the law allows, what a judge might do, or to advocate for you personally.

In a family law case, a mediator helps both parties, and his or her main goal is to encourage them to reach an agreement. In some cases, whether the mediator is an attorney or not, they even attempt to draft the separation agreement themselves, with varying degrees of success.

Because a mediator, even if he or she is an attorney, isn't acting in that capacity, it's often really helpful to work with an attorney as well. You don't have to take your attorney with you to mediation, but it's a good idea to meet with one both before and after mediation takes place.

Before mediation, the attorney can go over the law in Virginia with you and help you understand your rights and entitlements under the law. The attorney can run guideline child and spousal support, and help you articulate a range of acceptable outcomes, so that you don't go into mediation blindly.

After mediation, the attorney can review, revise, and/or draft the separation agreement. Keep in mind that a separation agreement, once signed, is virtually impossible, so you'll want to make sure you get it right from the beginning. One of the big risks we see of working with mediators, especially non-attorney mediators, is that they do a terrible job of drafting agreements.

The way we see it, a divorce attorney's job is two-fold: it includes (1) getting your divorce, and (2) minimizing the possibility of disruptive, expensive problems coming up later on down the line. Because mediators often aren't attorneys (and, even if they are, they aren't working in a mediated case as an attorney), they often don't go to court over these agreements.

They're not aware, in a broader sense, of the problems that can arise or how to draft an agreement to sidestep them. Their drafting is sometimes unclear or ambiguous, which creates problems, too, because the parties to the agreement don't have the same understanding of what the agreement requires them to do.

The second part – the problems later part – is where mediators often get tripped up. But it doesn't really make sense to save money on your divorce now, only to have super expensive problems arise post-divorce, does it? Consulting with an attorney can help you minimize the possibility of those kinds of problems coming up.

Am I a good candidate for mediation?

For many couples, mediation makes sense. In other cases, though, it can be less ideal. Specifically, if yours is an abusive relationship, mediation might not make sense.

Abuse – especially abuse suffered over a period of many years – can cause a lot of psychological damage. Mediation means that you're going into the process of negotiating a result in your own divorce without the assistance of an attorney to represent your interests. If you've been bulldozed throughout your marriage, not only will your soon-to-be ex attempt to do this in mediation, but (1) it's not the mediator's job to stop him, and (2) he may even try harder than usual if he feels his tactics aren't immediately working in the way that he has grown accustomed to.

There's an uneven balance of power between the two of you, and that's exacerbated by the stress of the divorce. Even if you're in therapy currently and working through your feelings, mediation is going to be a vulnerable position for you to be in. You would likely be in much better shape if you had a real advocate on your side.

I just can't afford an attorney. What would you advise?

It's not like anyone is out there trying to represent themselves because they think it'll be fun. No – women try to represent themselves because they don't feel like they have any other option.

There are very few attorneys – if any – who'll take an entire case on pro bono. Legal Aid is sometimes an option, but generally only for uncontested cases (cases where no litigation is involved), and even then there are very, very strict income guidelines. There is no question that there's a gap between the need for attorneys and the ability to afford to hire one.

If you can't afford to hire an attorney, I would still advise you to at least meet with one – maybe even more than once. You can have a separation agreement you drafted (or one drafted for you by a mediator) reviewed by an attorney. Likewise, if you were drafting your own pleadings (complaint, final decree of divorce, etc), you could also have those documents reviewed.

You don't have to retain an attorney (more on this in a minute) to meet with one, so this can be a cost effective way to still consult with an attorney and find out where there might be any issues. It's definitely better than nothing and has the potential to save you a lot of time, money, and frustration.

Chapter 2

I need to hire a family law attorney.

There are really only a few categories of cases where it's going to be even remotely possible to represent yourself – and, even then, there are a lot of risks involved, as we discussed in Chapter 1.

As you can probably also imagine, there are lots of categories of cases where it would be inadvisable to represent yourself. Let's talk about those cases.

What types or categories of cases would suggest that a lawyer is required?

- Custody/visitation is contested

- Spousal support is contested

- When you don't know the extent of the assets/liabilities

- Where your husband refuses to sign (or you refuse to sign) a separation agreement

- When your access to the marital money has been cut off unexpectedly

- When there's verbal, emotional, or physical abuse (the imbalance in power in relationships with an abusive dynamic can make negotiation difficult or impossible)

- Where you suspect that the children have been abused

- When one party is spending or wasting marital assets or increasing debt

- Where a relocation or deployment is coming up

- Where school enrollment is an issue

It's not an exhaustive list, but it's a start. In general, it's going to be unwise to represent yourself in a contested case, meaning one where you and your ex aren't able to reach an agreement. That doesn't mean, of course, that in uncontested cases – cases where the parties have been able to reach an agreement – that they got there easily or without some back and forth. In most cases, some amount of negotiation is required.

In any case, as we discussed in Chapter 1, drafting and negotiating a separation agreement is already fairly difficult. But, if one of you refuses to sign an agreement, or you have a big issue holding up the agreement, you may have no other option than to enlist an attorney to help you. A divorce can't be finalized with issues still left unresolved, so whether the attorney moves settlement discussions forward or litigates on your behalf, you and your soon-to-be ex are going to have to achieve some sort of final resolution on every issue.

Some issues are uglier or more complicated than others. In general, spousal support and custody and visitation are some of the biggest 'wild card' issues that can come up in a divorce or custody case. In general, other issues – like division of the retirement and the sale/refinance/disposition of the marital residence – are less complicated because what the court would do in these general situations is fairly well established.

Just because you hire an attorney doesn't mean that your case is going to court!

Of course, just because you're entitled to half of the marital share of his retirement doesn't mean that he'll willingly give it up! (In fact, many husbands tell their wives that they absolutely will not give them their share of the retirement.) Having an attorney involved in these cases can be helpful, too. Not only can your attorney advocate for you (rather than you doing so yourself), but his attorney can explain to him the way the law works and that it would not be a good use of his time or money to take this issue to trial. Though many people think that it's best if their ex is unrepresented, we often find that having attorneys on both sides helps achieve a resolution more quickly than the alternative.

Just because it's not easy to reach an immediate resolution does not mean that you're doomed to litigate in court. In fact, in most cases, we're able to smooth the way to reach a negotiated resolution – though we're still on hand to litigate in the event that attempts to settle fail.

"So, you're saying if I have one of these issues, I'll have to hire an attorney."

No one is going to force you to hire an attorney. Technically, the law allows you to represent yourself in any divorce or custody action in the Commonwealth.

I'm not telling you what you absolutely have to do, I'm just making recommendations based on my general experience in the level of difficulty in these types of cases.

It's not just a question of difficulty (though difficulty is relevant, especially if you haven't handled too many family law cases yourself) but also of the outcome you'll achieve and the cost you'll pay. Outcomes can be measured tangibly and intangibly, in the sense that the black and white letter of your agreement (or court order) matters, but also in the sense that your ability to be able to coparent together will be relevant even post divorce, if you have children in common. The cost, too, can be measured in more than one way. It's not just a question of the dollars you'll spend, though of course those dollars are important to you, but it's also the toll that the divorce takes on your mental and physical health in the meantime.

In almost every case, but certainly in cases that present some of these more complicated issues, a well chosen attorney can help improve the overall outcome of the case and decrease the total costs, while managing some of the more difficult aspects for you.

Can I get a pro bono lawyer, use Legal Aid, or get court appointed counsel in family law cases in Virginia?

So, you've accepted that you need a lawyer. What are your options? Money is tight, you're not sure how much it will cost, and you're overwhelmed.

Pro Bono Family Law Attorneys

There are a lot of misconceptions about attorneys doing pro bono work – namely, that there are these magical unicorn attorneys out there in the world that take on entire cases (complicated, difficult, litigated cases) absolutely free of charge.

That is, unfortunately, absolutely not the case.

The truth is that family law cases are difficult and incredibly stressful, and not just for the parties involved – for the attorneys, too. These cases, especially the litigated ones, represent countless hours and sleepless nights. It's not easy work, even though we do it every single day. It's very, very hard, and it doesn't get easier. Every single case is different and presents its own unique challenges. The law is constantly changing, too, and we have to keep up with it all.

Very few attorneys would take an entire case pro bono, at least in family law. (And by 'very few,' I mean that – as of the date of this writing – I know of exactly zero who will do it.) That's not to say that it's impossible to find someone, but I don't want to mislead you by making you think that this is something that regularly occurs. It is not.

I thought attorneys were required to do pro bono work.

It is true that attorneys are encouraged to offer free or discounted services to underserved populations – but, in Virginia at least, it is not a formal requirement. It is also not a requirement that, in order to help an underserved population, you take on an entire case for free from beginning to end.

Family law cases can take years and cost tens of thousands of dollars. At the beginning of a case, it can be difficult to tell what's involved, how long it will take, or how much it will cost. To ask an attorney to take on an entire case without any limitations whatsoever is a huge ask. For that reason, most attorneys will not offer to do it.

If an attorney does offer pro bono help, it's usually in a specific, limited capacity. For example, the Virginia Beach Bar Association sponsors the CLASS program (which stands for Concerned Lawyers Advocating Spousal Safety). Members of the bar association are encouraged to volunteer their time to the CLASS program, and appear on behalf of people looking to secure protective orders on Friday mornings in the Virginia Beach Juvenile Court.

It's possible, too, that an attorney would, say, offer a consultation for free (though many family law attorneys don't do this, as a general rule) in a specific situation or offer to help with some narrow, focused part of the case – like, for example, preparing and propounding discovery, or representation at a pendente lite hearing – without taking on the entire case for no fee.

In our office, we consider our Monthly Divorce Seminars to be part of our pro bono work, and we've always offered fee waivers or scholarships to allow women to attend. (Though the seminar itself is not free, the attorneys are not paid for their time in presenting the seminars.)

You're welcome to call around to see whether an attorney would be willing to take your case pro bono, or even just meet with you on a pro bono basis. I don't want to be discouraging, but I also don't think that you are likely to be successful.

What about Legal Aid?

It is always worth a call to a Legal Aid office. In general, though, I find that Legal Aid attorneys are severely overworked already, and the income limits to qualify require that you be well below the poverty line. Many people, even people who desperately need access to these resources, do not qualify. Furthermore, even if they do qualify, most of the time the cases that Legal Aid is able to undertake are uncontested ones.

Why? Mostly because, by accepting uncontested cases only, they can help far more people with far less money. The money that might otherwise go towards one contested divorce might help 15-20 people get an uncontested divorce.

Even though Legal Aid can't represent everyone who walks through their doors, they do try to help. Many times, even in cases where they can't extend an offer of representation, the Legal Aid attorneys will try to do something to help. I can't say for certain whether that would be the case for you, but it's always worth a call to see whether there are any services available to you.

What about military legal or JAG attorneys?

Military legal services are complicated. In general, because of ethical rules regarding conflict of interests, the first party who gets to military legal will get advice. If you go to military legal after your husband, you may find that they tell you that they are conflicted out of even talking to you. You may be able to seek legal counsel from a different branch of service, but, at any rate, the service that military legal can offer you is limited in the extreme.

Keep in mind that military attorneys, JAG attorneys, are not licensed to practice law in the Commonwealth of Virginia. They practice military law. They can't take family law cases and can't appear in court.

Why? Well, there are basically two parts to having a license to practice law in a particular state. You have to pass the bar exam, and then you have to be formally admitted to practice in the state (or, in our case, Commonwealth). Virginia attorneys have licenses issued by the Virginia State Bar, and we take continuing education classes each year in order to keep our licenses active.

Generally speaking, a military service member passes a bar exam and joins the military. They are assigned a permanent duty station, which may or may not be in the same state where they passed the bar. In any case, though, they don't apply to the state bar association for a license; they practice military law, and have a military license. They appear in front of military courts, but not state courts.

Does that mean they don't give divorce advice? Unfortunately, no. The problem, though, is that sometimes they unknowingly give the wrong advice. They often also have a bias towards the active duty military service member, rather than the spouse.

A military JAG attorney should not draft a separation agreement, but that does not mean that it has never happened before. **If a JAG attorney drafts an agreement for you (or on behalf of your husband), you should not sign that agreement unless and until you have it reviewed by a practicing, licensed, Virginia family law attorney.**

You may choose to consult with a JAG attorney (if only so that your husband has the unsettling experience of showing up to a JAG office to find that you beat him to it), but you should also keep in mind that their advice may not be accurate. It's best to talk to someone with a Virginia license, who has experience representing clients in Virginia courts, and who can help you no matter what twists and turns your case may take.

Can I get a court appointed attorney in a family law case?

In a word... no. Constitutionally, the only right you have to counsel is where your liberty is threatened – so, basically, a criminal case where you risk jail time. Even in those cases, you have to lack the resources to hire an attorney yourself, and then you have to accept whomever is appointed as your public defender.

Much like Legal Aid attorneys, public defenders are overworked and underpaid, and often lack the time to give each case the kind of attention that an attorney in private practice would be able to dedicate.

There is no Constitutional right to a public defender in a family law case, so there is no option for any kind of court appointed counsel regardless of your income level.

How much do attorneys cost?

So, if there's not another alternative to hiring an attorney – what, exactly, are you in for? If you're anything like me, you want to know what to expect before you go too far down any road in particular. How much does it cost to hire an attorney?

Is there a free consultation?

Generally speaking, family law attorneys don't do free consultations.

You've probably heard plenty of ads for attorneys promising free consultations but, by and large, those are personal injury attorneys. Personal injury attorneys are pretty different for a couple of reasons. For one thing, they can take a contingent fee – you know, the whole 'we don't get paid unless we win' thing. Personal injury lawyers often take anywhere between 30-50% of a final settlement in a case, depending on whether the case was resolved out of court or in court.

Personal injury attorneys are looking for high dollar cases. The more they win in a lawsuit, the greater the fee they take away from each case. So, they WANT to encourage you to come in and meet with them. They'll even come to you, at your home or in the hospital! Why? They get a big chunk of what you recover.

Personal injury attorneys are hunting for valuable cases. Family law attorneys, on the other hand, aren't looking for the most lucrative cases.

In family law, it's considered unethical to take a contingent fee. We cannot take a case based off of getting a certain percentage of the overall settlement amount. You wouldn't want it anyway! Can you imagine each attorney – yours and your husband's – taking even 20% of everything you've accumulated in your marriage?

Instead, family law attorneys bill hourly, so the total amount your case costs will depend on how long it takes to resolve. In the Hampton Roads area, where our firm is located, most attorneys charge somewhere between $300-500 an hour. In more urban areas, like Northern Virginia, the average hourly rate is usually higher; in more rural areas, or further west, the hourly rates might be lower.

All of our cases 'cost' the same in the sense that every single client is paying the same hourly rate for the same attorney. We're not trying to scour Hampton Roads for the most valuable family law cases, either. We look at a consultation differently.

It's not an audition for a client, it's an information-gathering session. We try to focus as much as possible on providing value to each and every client, so that they have an understanding of their rights and entitlements under the law, and the tools they need to come up with a blueprint for how to move their case forward. It's highly individualized and specific. For that reason, we – and most family law attorneys in our area – do charge for our initial consultations.

Retainers and Retainer Agreements

We bill hourly, as we've said, but in general most of our work is done on retainers. A retainer is an amount of money that is paid by a client into a trust (or escrow) account. The money is the client's, and stays the client's, until it is earned by the attorney.

We bill in increments of 0.1 of an hour depending on how long each thing takes to accomplish. Whether we're writing emails, sending letters, drafting pleadings, appearing in court, talking on the telephone, or participating in a settlement conference, it is all billed according to the attorney's hourly rate.

Usually, the retainer fee that you pay – basically, the amount of money that you need to come up with up front for the attorney to take your case – is based on the type of case and the level of complexity involved. A separation agreement case usually starts at $2,500-3,500, while a contested divorce case can run $7,500 and up.

Keep in mind that a retainer fee is not a flat fee, nor is it an estimate of how much your case will cost overall. It's only an amount that you place in trust at the beginning of the case in order for the attorney to undertake representation of you. If your trust account runs out while the case is still ongoing, you'll be expected to replenish your trust account.

Most attorneys use a retainer agreement – basically, a legal contract that describes the rights and obligations of each party – to govern the relationship between attorney and client. The retainer agreement will explain what is billed, how it is billed, when it is billed, along with any minimum billing conventions and minimum trust account balances. At our office, we call it a 'minimum fee security deposit' which basically just means the minimum amount that you are expected to maintain in your trust account at all times. You're not expected to maintain your trust account at the same level as your retainer fee, but you would be expected to maintain that predetermined minimum balance.

In the event that there is money left over in your trust account when your case is concluded, that money should be refunded to you. You should read your retainer agreement before you sign, like you would any legal contract, and ask any questions that you have about how the firm functions before you retain.

Hourly Fees

Family law attorneys almost always bill hourly. As a result, the best way to compare costs between attorneys is to look at their hourly rate.

A retainer fee isn't necessarily a representation of how expensive or inexpensive a case will be. An hourly rate, on the other hand, helps you understand how many hours of legal work you've paid up front to receive.

An attorney's hourly rate is often directly proportional to their level of experience. Newer attorneys are often at the lower end of the spectrum, while the more experienced attorneys charge more per hour.

'More experienced' doesn't always mean 'the absolute best', though. Whether you choose to hire an attorney who has been in practice a few years, a million years, or somewhere in between, you'll want to follow our guide to help make sure you choose the right attorney for YOU. Plenty of attorneys out there have been doing a mediocre job for a really long time, and plenty of up-and-coming, hungry younger attorneys are poised to launch impressive careers. Years in practice matters, but so do a lot of other factors.

Paralegals and Other Office Professionals

Paralegals are an important – and often undervalued – resource, too. If there's anyone in a family law case who can help save you money, it's your paralegal. Don't underestimate her.

A paralegal is like a nurse. They do SO much of the valuable work, and often for far, far less than the doctor. Although each attorney/paralegal relationship is different, many paralegals take on a fair amount of the heavy lifting for their attorneys, so that the attorney can focus on the most important tasks at hand. Paralegals draft documents, formulate correspondence, schedule hearings, arrange for service of process, meet with clients, and often a whole lot more. Their hourly rates are often significantly less than the attorney's hourly rate, too, so their participation can constitute a huge amount of savings for the client, without compromising on quality or knowledge of the law.

Don't forget to consider the paralegal and be sure to ask any attorney with whom you meet about her paralegal, including what tasks she delegates to her, and what her hourly rate is. A strong attorney/client relationship translates to savings for the client.

Payment Plans

You are also likely to find that most family law attorneys don't offer payment plans. You can probably see how chaotic that could easily become. If a client can't pay the initial retainer amount, and instead arranges to pay it monthly over a period of time, what happens if the retainer amount is insufficient to allow the case to continue?

Remember: retainer fees are not an estimate of total overall costs in a case. They're not flat fees, either. When the retainer runs out, the client is expected to replenish their trust account. You can see how, if the client is already on a payment plan, this could spiral out of control.

At our firm, we're advocates for women. Representing women is important to us. But we're not a charitable institution. We don't have state or government funding. We're a private law firm, and, like you, we're just regular people who go to work every day to earn a paycheck so that we can pay our student loans and our mortgages, take care of our kids, and keep the lights on. Just like you, we need to be paid, and we can't afford to go to work for free.

If you're experiencing financial hardship, it's a good idea to have a one on one conversation with your lawyer about how to handle your case moving forward.

Conclusion

Just like it's important to understand what your rights and entitlements are under the law, it's also important to understand what to expect when it comes to working with an attorney. For most people, hiring an attorney is not something that they do every day.

If you have worked with an attorney before, chances are good that it wasn't a family law attorney – and, as you've probably already realized, different types of attorneys take cases and bill their clients differently.

Even if you have used a family law attorney before, if it was a long time ago, or if it was in another state, you may find that things are different now, in Virginia. It's always important to double check your assumptions, not make decisions based on your fears, and to make every effort to get up to date, Virginia specific information that relates to your specific situation.

You're in the right place.

Chapter 3

Finding a Family Law Attorney

So, now that you've established that (1) you need an attorney, and (2) that you understand how family law attorneys bill their clients in divorce and custody cases, it may be time to start actually looking for a lawyer.

Do you enjoy research? I do... sometimes. But, even in the cases where I'm enjoying myself the most (which would probably not be when researching attorneys), I prefer to have a little extra information to guide me.

Take Disney World for instance. You might love planning trips (I know I do!) but then, when you get down into the details, it's easy to feel overwhelmed. You want some insider knowledge. Someone who has been there before, and can tell you which resort is best – or maybe you prefer to stay off the Disney property, to keep your costs low. What happens with parking? Is there a shuttle? How often? Where can you make reservations to eat? Does the Bippity Boppity Boutique REALLY cost $250 per kid? Because that's just insane. So, maybe you contact a travel agent who specializes in Disney World.

Maybe you talk to a friend, too – but, then again, maybe not – because what your Aunt Carol experienced at Disney back in 1996 is going to be a little different from what you come across today. It's hard to substitute information that you glean from internet searches (from questionable sources) versus what you can learn from someone who has specialized knowledge.

In Virginia, it's considered unethical for a lawyer to call themselves an expert or to indicate that they specialize in a particular area of law. I'm not calling myself an expert or a specialist, but I am a family law attorney, practicing in Virginia, representing women exclusively, for an extended period of time. I do think I have some insight that could help you as you begin to research family law attorneys in Virginia.

You are the only person who should be choosing a lawyer to represent you.

There is a lot of misleading and confusing information out there. Let me help you make sense of it all.

Directory Sites and Referral Sites

There are a number of websites out there that compile lists of attorneys for you – like FindLaw.com, Attorneys.com, LegalMatch.com, Justia.com and even Avvo. You may be familiar with some – or all – of these websites.

If you search for the city you live in and divorce attorneys, you are likely to get results from one or more of these sites. Some of them just have a list of attorneys and their contact information; others are 'referral' sites, which means that they'll gather your information and refer you to an attorney.

In many cases, whether you're on a directory site or seeking answers on a referral site, the results you will see are what the lawyers have paid for you to see. The top attorneys that will show up on a directory site's list are the ones who've paid for ads. To appear in the top one or two spots, the attorneys pay a premium fee. To appear further down the list, the attorney or firm will likely pay a lesser fee.

Likewise, on a referral site, where your information is forwarded to an attorney who will respond to you, the attorney usually pays for that service. The site generates leads, and the law firm pays them for those leads as a way to generate new business.

These sites certainly have their uses. It can be helpful to look through a list of names and firms, especially when you're in the beginning stages of gathering information. But it can also be misleading, and it's important that you know exactly what you're seeing when you use these sites. You're seeing ads that are designed to influence your behavior and decision making.

Not that there's anything wrong with ads! When you're in the market for a product or service, it can be super helpful to see advertisements that help you make a decision you're already going to make. The problem occurs not when advertising is used, but when a person using it misunderstands the ad. You may think, for example, that seeing a certain attorney on top of a list at FindLaw means that this person is the #1 family law attorney in your area. It's certainly designed to look that way, after all. And while that person may (or may not) be an excellent attorney, there's a difference between doing the research and choosing that person to represent you based on your independent assessment of their strengths and weaknesses, and being manipulated into thinking that there's some sort of ranking process happening here.

SuperLawyers, Best of ..., and Other Attorney Awards

Keep in mind, too, that many attorney 'awards' often work similarly. While there may be an element of merit to the award itself, there's often a lot of marketing behind the scenes.

For some awards, in order to use the specific, branded 'badge' indicating that the lawyer has received the award, the lawyer (or firm) has to pay a fee to the company that issues the award. It's a marketing expense for the attorney, because the casual observer thinks that the attorney has done something award-worthy; it's a revenue generator for the company sponsoring the award. It's an interesting symbiosis.

That's not to say, again, that there's no merit involved. There often is. At least, it was that attorney's name that came up, or who was nominated by their peers, or whatever it happens that the company used for its criteria to determine who received the award. It's just that, by the time the consumer sees it, it's also become a little distorted. You don't pay? You can't display the badge on your website. Oh – but for just $249.99, you can also have this lovely plaque for your wall, so all your clients can be dazzled by your brilliance.

Just, you know … be aware.

Other awards, like the 'best of' awards you see locally by a newspaper or radio station or magazine, derive a substantial amount of income from the advertisements placed by would-be winners. Again, it generates revenue. It's also often the result of a huge marketing effort by the firm. Once they've put their names forward for consideration, they'll undertake a huge campaign imploring their followers to vote for them to win.

It's not judged impartially by some independent, unbiased criteria. It's not an objective determination of the 'best of' anything. It's a popularity contest, undertaken by those who willingly put their names forward, and most diligently convinced their supporters to vote for them.

And then, because they paid a teeny tiny extra fee, their names can appear in bold, at the top of the list, conveniently next to a half page color ad displaying the lovely mahogany desk, many leatherbound books, and beautiful, smiling receptionist that will greet you when you schedule your divorce consultation with them.

Hey, to each their own! And, if I'm being honest, I've appeared on a few of those lists myself over the years. We all have, I think. Once upon a time, it used to be really important. And, I admit, I'm still flattered to be included. (And, if, after the date of publication of this book, I am no longer included, I won't wonder why.) But I also think it's important that you know, in advance, that the people at the top, the people in bold, the people who paid extra to be highlighted, might look like they've been selected because of their expertise, when in fact it's as a result of the strength of their marketing budget. Or insecurity. Or both.

I'll say it again: you are the only person who should be choosing an attorney to represent you. Don't let them do it for you!

Attorney Websites, Reviews, Social Media, and Online Presence

These days, one of the best ways to learn about an attorney or law practice is to look at their website, including their reviews and their social media accounts.

Attorney Websites

You can tell a lot about an attorney or firm by their website. Does the website speak to you and what you're going through, or does it seem to exist only to glorify the attorney?

Read the attorney's bio. Read all of the attorney's bios. Do you feel like this is a person that you could sit across a table from and have a real, honest conversation about some of the most private parts of your life? Can you talk about the health of your marriage? Your sex life? Your finances? Your parenting? Drug or alcohol addiction? Your fears and concerns for the future?

The right attorney for you isn't just a 'pitbull,' it's someone that you think will have your best interests at heart. Who you can have a real conversation with about your goals, and then work backwards to create a tailored plan for how to achieve them. Who'll treat your life, your assets, your children, the way she would want her own to be treated.

It's not too much to expect from an attorney. You're coming to them at an intensely challenging time of your life, and you need to know that you have someone in your corner who will listen to you, answer your questions, help you see the opportunities and alternatives available to you, advocate for you, and help ensure that you receive what you are entitled to receive from your spouse.

Does the attorney's website help you? Does it educate you? Does it speak to you? Or is it just a stage for the attorney to showcase his or her professional achievements? Do you have a sense of the attorney or firm's ethos? Do you like what you see?

You'll want to get a sense of the larger site and also of the individual attorney's bio. If you don't have a particular attorney in mind, read all of the bios. What stands out? Do you feel more or less comfortable about the prospect of spending an hour in their company?

Personally, I'd take points off any website that featured Lady Justice (you know, the blindfolded Grecian woman holding a set of scales?), Corinthian columns, or the scales of justice – it's just too cliché. But you may not be quite as averse to those things as I am.

Reviews

Have you looked at any reviews on the firm or the attorney? You probably should. It's a good idea to get a sense of what people are saying about the attorney or firm you're considering.

What do the bad reviews say?

That's not to say, of course, that you should exclude someone just because there is a negative review. Negative reviews happen. Just like people in every other profession, there are good and bad lawyers. Both good lawyers and bad lawyers sometimes get bad reviews. In some cases, the bad reviews are truly because the lawyer is bad.

Bad reviews can happen to good lawyers, too, though. Keep in mind that lawyers – all lawyers, not just family lawyers – tend to see people during life crises. It's not a strong moment for a lot of people. There are a lot of emotions involved. And, sometimes, regardless of a lawyer's best efforts, things don't go the way the client thinks that they should. It's possible that there were unreasonable expectations. I mean, it's your life, your money, your kids – it's easy to have unreasonable expectations, especially when you're already going through a pretty traumatic life event.

Actually look at the bad review, though. Read what it says. Does it sound like the person who wrote it is careful, logical, and reasonable? Does it sound like they're telling the truth? Are they blaming the lawyer for something that wasn't the lawyer's fault? Are they just in a really bad situation? Or is there something more serious going on?

It's important to understand where people might be coming from. In general, people who are in the process of getting a divorce or going through a custody case are dealing with an incredible amount of fear. They're angry, overwhelmed, tired, fearful, anxious, depressed, hurt – the list goes on and on. In many cases, they aren't taking great care of their mental health; maybe, they don't even know that they need to. When people are scared or feel backed into a corner, they can lash out. They can apportion blame. They can make decisions that, under the normal light of day, don't make sense. It's not a personality flaw; it's a really crippling set of circumstances.

Don't just look at an overall star rating, either. Actually get in there and read the reviews. Sometimes, there will be a review that is just a one star rating and no comment – is it a competing law firm? In other cases, there might be a review but the person (most places, like Google and Facebook require that you use your name; you can't leave an anonymous review) isn't a client, or, if they are, the firm can't identify them. Did the firm respond with a "We're not sure you're a client at all?" response. Sometimes, people writing reviews make mistakes and attribute a bad review in the wrong place, or bash someone out of context for something unrelated to the quality of their work.

In other cases, the bad reviews can actually be good reviews! One of our one-star reviews on Google is from a husband! We didn't represent him – we represent women exclusively – but his wife got such a good result when she was represented by one of our attorneys that he took to social media to bash us! So, is that REALLY a 1 star review? You can be the judge, but it sounds to me more like a bad case of sour grapes. You can read it here (and also on Google):

> *My ex-wife is represented by this firm. With no regard to the damage that they caused to my children, they enabled her to petition the court to remove my custody of my children from me simply because they were getting paid to. If you're a self-pitying, immature, and selfish woman bent on vengeance, this is your firm, ladies.*

So, really, all that to say that it's not a question of whether there are any bad reviews at all. Most businesses, ours included, have some reviews that aren't glowingly positive. (And, honestly, as a consumer, I'd be a little suspicious of a place where there were no negative reviews. How is that humanly possible?) The question isn't "Are there any negative reviews at all?", but, rather, "How does the lawyer respond to negative reviews?" and "How accurate and reasonable do I think this feedback actually is?"

What do the good reviews say?

Read the good reviews, too! (I know – it's tempting to just look at the bad ones!) Does one lawyer at the firm stand out from the others? Are any of the reviewers describing cases like yours? Do the reviews say that the attorney responded quickly? (This is important, because one of the biggest complaints that clients tend to have about attorneys relates to their responsiveness; you want an attorney who'll respond to you in a timely fashion!) Do the reviews say that the client understood the process? That they felt prepared? That the attorney was good in court? That she handled negotiations effectively?

There are a lot of things that a person can praise, but what, specifically, they choose to pinpoint can tell you a lot about the attorney and how you'll feel if you hire that same person to represent you.

Compare the good reviews with the bad. See whether there are similarities and differences. Carefully consider and weigh the reviews against each other.

For your purposes, all reviews are good reviews – because, if you take the good with the bad, it paints a clearer picture for you about what you can expect, which will help you make a better decision when it comes time to hire an attorney to represent you.

Consider how the attorney or firm responds to feedback, too.

It's not just whether there are good reviews or bad reviews on the attorney or firm. It's also a question of how they responded to the feedback.

Do they graciously accept the bad feedback, suggesting an improvement in their processes? Do they suggest that the client come in to discuss the situation further? Do they respond inappropriately or blame the client? Are they sympathetic and professional or rude and callous? Basically, do they add fuel to the fire or try to improve the situation? Does the response make you feel that the review is more or less accurate?

If the review is ignored, that says something, too, assuming that the review has been there long enough that the attorney has had a reasonable opportunity to respond. It's good customer service to respond appropriately to a bad review. An attorney or firm who doesn't respond to bad feedback is telling you something, too. Do they not care? Are they too lazy to respond? Is there no defense to the allegations leveled against them? Are they so un-savvy that they don't know HOW to respond? It may not be possible to say, but it is clear that not responding is not good, either.

Keep in mind, though, that an attorney may be limited in how he or she may be able to respond, because the client is still protected by confidentiality. Even though the client may choose to share information that would otherwise be covered under attorney/client privilege, the attorney may not share that information.

An appropriate response to a bad review is important!

Nextdoor and Other Referral Apps

There may be other apps that you can use to get a recommendation for a good lawyer, too. I've seen a lot of posts looking for lawyers – or at least, looking for recommendations from other locals who may have used a particular kind of lawyer – in Nextdoor pretty often, right up there next to all the lost dogs.

In the olden days, there was Angie's List (which, apparently, now is called Angi), but there may be other similar apps you can use, especially if you'd rather have others recommend a lawyer rather than using Google to search for one on your own.

Social Media

Almost everyone is on social media these days – lawyers included. So, while you're checking out the latest reels on TikTok, you can also do some research on your potential divorce lawyer.

We all participate in social media to different degrees, but you should be able to get a feel for the attorney and/or the firm's personality, ethos, and worldview. You can also find out about any upcoming events, speaking engagements, publications, court cases, or other accomplishments of the firm and/or the individual lawyers!

On social media, you can also use local groups for referrals. There are a ton of mom groups out there, and I find they're often full of requests for recommendations for lawyers. Though I recommend, in general, not taking legal advice from a non lawyer, a referral is an entirely different matter. See who is recommended. Maybe you won't hire those people, but at least it's a good starting point for some research.

Word of Mouth

Never underestimate a direct referral, either. We all know someone who got divorced or went through a custody case. Ask them! Whether they were happy or unhappy with their representation, they can likely give you some really valuable information.

Ask what they liked, what they didn't like. Ask them what they'd do differently or what they wish they had known. Ask them about their ultimate result. Was anything surprising? What about custody? Are there any clever provisions put in place that helped make the arrangement more manageable? There's nothing like hearing from a real life person who has been there and done that already.

Once you've gone through these steps, you should have some names on a list, whether it's firms generally or specific attorneys. And now you're ready to start the next part of the process: actually choosing someone to represent you.

Chapter 4

Choosing a Family Law Attorney

It's time to start making decisions! You could Google forever – and question and re-question your thought process – but, at some point, it's time to pull the trigger.

First step? Schedule a consultation.

Scheduling a Consultation

Does it make you nervous? I think that's pretty normal. I hear pretty often that the idea of calling an attorney's office – and, worse, sitting in front of them! – is pretty anxiety-inducing.

I'd start out on the attorney's website. Some firms will have an online feature that you can use to schedule a consultation; others may require you to actually call in.

Not sure what to expect or what information you'll be asked to provide? That's fair. I can't tell you what might happen if you call into anybody else's office, but I can give you some insight into what might happen if you called into ours. Our receptionists are supposed to ask specific questions to make sure that we get all the information we need to make sure you get the help you need.

Everyone's different, of course. Some people tell us their whole life stories, while others prefer to just schedule a consultation without giving hardly any information at all. It's definitely a vulnerable time, so, either way, it's completely understandable.

A couple suggestions, though. Before you call in, especially if you're worried about your husband finding out that you've consulted with a divorce attorney, it's a good idea to create a spouse safe email.

Not every situation is dangerous, but in some cases it is. And, even in others where violence is not a concern, you might not want him to know yet that you're talking to an attorney about a potential divorce.

A spouse safe email is one that your soon-to-be ex doesn't know about. We usually recommend creating a new gmail account – these are regarded as some of the most secure – in order to receive case-related correspondence. Whether you visit our website and request a copy of one of our free books or reports, register to attend a divorce or custody webinar, or schedule a consultation (or some combination of all of the above), we'll ask you to provide an email address. It's a good idea to be prepared for this up front, and to have an email account already created, especially if you have security concerns with the one that you generally use. (And then, don't forget to check it!)

Similarly, if you have concerns about your phone number, make sure to let the office know how and/or when it can be used. If you don't want any phone calls, say so. It's probably not practical (or even necessary) to go to the time, trouble, and expense to get a burner phone, but we could communicate by email instead if you're worried. It's definitely something to mention.

Also – payment. Most family law offices charge a fee for an initial consultation. In our office, we also ask for prepayment of that fee, so that we can officially reserve the attorney's time. (Don't worry, though: it's completely refundable in case you change your mind or need to cancel or reschedule for any reason at all.)

Again, this is a way that your soon-to-be ex may find out what's going on. If you have a shared checking account or credit card account that you normally use, this is something to be aware of. If you're not ready to arouse suspicion, you may want to use an account that is yours separately. It's not ridiculous to even get a credit card or bank account in your own name; at some point in this process, you'll probably need or want to anyway! But if you can't, or don't want to, or just want to go ahead and schedule your consultation NOW, not after you've had a chance to jump through all these extra hoops, that's fine too.

One thing that we recommend when there are shared bank accounts (but our prospective client doesn't want to give away her intentions just yet) is that you purchase a Visa gift card and load it with the amount of money you need to pay for the consultation. Then, you can run that gift card like a normal credit or debit card, but it won't show up in the transaction record on your bank account or your credit card statement.

You could also use cash, but that can be difficult if the office (like ours) requires prepayment. If that's what you want or need to do, though, just let us know and we can make an exception for you. Checks aren't preferred; we usually do a ten day hold on them to make sure that they're able to be processed. So, if you want to use a check, you just need to build in enough time to accommodate the ten day hold. A money order is also fine, but there are fees associated; we most commonly see these for retainer payments, rather than for the consultation fee. But it's up to you!

70

The most important thing is to consider the record that you're making and, if you're not ready for your husband to find out, to have a plan in advance for how to protect yourself. So, now – the phone call.

Calling the Office

What information will you be asked to provide? How much is too much? If it makes you feel any better, we've literally heard it all before, and no one is judging you. No one thinks you're stupid if, in the moment, you feel like you need to unburden yourself; likewise, no one is going to ask you to give a lot of detail that you're not willing or comfortable providing over the phone to a near complete stranger.

What types of questions will you hear?

- **Can I ask your name?**

- **How did you hear about us?**

- **Where do you live?**

- **Do you have an upcoming court date that we should know about?**

- **Would you mind telling us a little more about why you called our office today?**

That's... about it. We need to know about, for example, where you live, because that will tell us where a court case might be filed. Upcoming court dates, likewise, help us make sure that we've assigned you to an attorney who practices in your court and who is available on any date that might already be scheduled.

As far as providing more information about why you're calling in, you can keep it simple. 'Divorce,' is both one word, and a more than adequate answer. If you want to expound more, feel free. We're used to that, too.

After that, we'll work towards helping make sure that we come up with a solution for you. If you're ready to schedule a consultation, we'll look at your availability and the attorney's availability and help you get something scheduled. If you're not quite ready yet, we'll help you register for a seminar or get a hard copy of one of our books out to you in the mail.

If you already have an attorney in mind, we can schedule you with that attorney. If you'd prefer to have us match you with who's most appropriate based on what's happening in your case, we can try to do that too. If you want to get in immediately and you just want the first available appointment, say no more! While I can understand feeling like you should choose your attorney yourself, you really can't go wrong with any one of our attorneys.

We'll also give you some information about the consult fee, what to expect in terms of next steps, and answer any questions that you might have about the attorney, our office, or what to expect. If you have questions you want to ask, you should feel free to ask them.

There are no stupid questions. Ask! You're going through a lot, and you shouldn't make it worse on yourself because you're too intimidated to ask questions. We're used to it. We've heard it before. Promise.

The Initial Consultation: What to Expect

So, you've scheduled a consultation. What next? It's time to meet with the attorney one-on-one.

How do I prepare for a consultation?

It's smart to give some thought to what you want to say to the attorney before you find yourself in her office. It's not an easy experience for anyone. It's a difficult conversation. Admitting the depths of the difficulties you've experienced in your marriage is no easy feat. You might be surprised at how you are feeling or how you react in the moment, so it's a good idea to prepare a little bit beforehand so that you can make sure to get in everything you want to mention and every question you hope to ask.

This is a shocking, agonizing, painstaking process. You're human. As hurt or angry or frustrated or scared as you are, as done as you may feel with the situation as a whole, it's still a different ballgame once you start taking actual, formal, calculated steps to end it.

So, I think I'd start there.

1. Have a plan to deal with the emotions involved in your divorce and/or custody case.

While you can talk to your attorney about your emotions, your attorney isn't really trained to deal with these things. I'm always happy to talk about it, but then I wonder whether I give the best, most effective advice. Legally, I know what I'm talking about, and I feel very confident I can help you along a path that will lead you to the happily ever after you've envisioned.

I'm happy, too, to help you work through the emotional pieces, but I do think you're probably generally in better hands with a licensed mental health professional.

You're not crazy. I don't think you are. And, really, crazy people probably don't need therapy first and foremost – they need more serious medical intervention. You're a normal person going through abnormally challenging circumstances. To come out better, stronger, smarter on the other side, you'll want to enlist a team of professionals – including an attorney, but also, probably, including a therapist.

(Besides, attorneys can't bill your insurance.)

If you set this up beforehand, you'll be in a better position to deal with the challenges of your divorce, and that will put you ahead of the game.

2. Do some research about family law in Virginia.

Don't come in totally blind. Then you'll waste your hour getting the basics, and not get into the finer points as it relates to your case.

You don't have to do anything crazy – like go to law school – but it's a good idea to have a general understanding of basic principles before you meet with a lawyer.

Anything you don't understand you can ask the attorney about at your consultation, but you will probably find that there's a lot you understand just fine. That can help you frame your thoughts (and anticipate potential problems) so that you are ready to have a conversation.

Nothing that happens in the initial consultation can't be undone, but you are beginning to put the train on the tracks. What you say, how you react, and the picture you paint has a lot to do with the recommendations the attorney will make, the retainer she will give you, and what first steps she'll start to prepare you to take. You can pump the brakes, or put that train on a different set of tracks, but you'd be better served to start from the beginning with an idea of where you want to end up. A lot of that can come from having a degree of familiarity with the divorce process from the get-go.

3. Do some soul searching. What are your divorce or custody goals?

It's only natural to respond emotionally in situations like this. I know I would, if it were me. None of us are superhuman.

But I often find that, when I have plenty of time to prepare for something, to collect my thoughts, to compose my arguments, and to be able to most effectively articulate my feelings and expectations, things end up better. Sure, I can launch into an immediate discussion – but that's not when I'm at my best.

Probably you aren't, either.

And, if you're for sure headed down this path, it's a good idea to give it some consideration. Where do you want to wind up? What are your goals? If you could paint the perfect picture of what it's like to be you post-divorce, what would it look like? How do you get there?

Your attorney can help you with some of the procedural stuff, but you'll want to think about the personal, logistical, financial stuff. We're an equitable distribution state – not a community property state – but still, things will probably be divided somewhere close to 50/50. What 50% do you want? What compromises could you make that would put him in a more conciliatory frame of mind? What could induce you to go to court, and what considerations would keep you out of it?

4. Be prepared to hear your attorney's advice, whether it's what you want to hear or not.

You probably have some pretty strong feelings about the situation you're in. And you probably have some expectations surrounding what you feel you deserve – whether it's a certain amount of spousal support or a certain amount of parenting time.

Your attorney, though, will give you advice. Being attorneys, we can also always back up our advice with very sound reasoning, explanations regarding the court, current law, recent cases, and other information we have at our disposal (but that you might not).

Whether you like the advice you receive or not, sleep on it. Give it some thought. Have an open, honest discussion with your attorney – whether at a second consultation, or after you've retained. It takes time to process these things, and if you're overwhelmed, surprised, anxious, angry, or otherwise not in a good head space, you'll need to take even more time.

Don't be reactive. Listen. Think. And then, later, respond. Ask questions at any point, especially if you don't understand or what to hear the reasoning behind a particular recommendation.

If you don't trust the attorney's advice, get a second opinion. If two (or three or four) attorneys say some version of the same thing, you may feel better about trusting her. Sometimes, we have to give advice – or make recommendations, or give answers – that we know our clients won't like to hear. We don't make the laws. But it can be difficult to hear, and we completely understand that.

So, take the time. Do the soul searching. And be prepared to hear your attorney's recommendations.

What, exactly, happens in an initial consultation?

We get a lot of consultations that are scheduled, and then rescheduled, rescheduled again, and sometimes even flat out cancelled. I get it. It's scary. And coming in for a divorce consultation with a real lawyer can seem like a step that you may or may not be ready to take.

In the early days before you are for sure ready to move forward with divorce, there are good days and bad days. Bad days, where you fight and schedule divorce consultations, and good days, where you think maybe you could work on your issues and this might not be the end. Sometimes, it's all about marriage counseling and saving things for the sake of the children, and other days it seems too far gone to be saved.

This tug o' war is completely normal, and if you're in the throes of it right now, don't feel bad about it. We expect some uncertainty at this stage in the game, and we've seen it all before. We're not going to judge you if you aren't sure what you want, or even if you want things to be over. We're here to give you advice and guidance, not to push you in any particular direction.

Well, normally, in an initial consultation, you and an attorney sit together in the attorney's office, and you have a chance to tell your story, ask any questions you might have, and work with the attorney to identify your goals so that you can begin to talk through any options you might have to move your case forward.

In our office, we offer consultations over the phone, Zoom, or in person in our Newport News, Chesapeake, and Virginia Beach offices.

In many consultations, it's a question of options. Depending on your risk tolerance, on your specific goals, you might make different choices for how to proceed. It's not like we tell you that there's only one way forward, and you have to go that way. In most cases, you'll have some choices – do you negotiate first, or do the circumstances warrant you going ahead and filing for divorce now? Do you try to negotiate custody first, or do you handle it all together? Is relocation, or your divorce, the main priority today?

There are often lots of options, and lots of issues, that are connected and interrelated.

In an initial consultation, we are looking at your case to give you advice, to educate you, and to help make sure you can make the best decisions possible.

What should I bring with me?

Any documents you have! Credit card statements, mortgage statements, existing court orders, prenuptial agreements, custody agreements, whatever – we may not be able to look at everything in the first hour, but it'll help us begin to figure out what the issues are.

When in doubt, bring it! We can sort through to find the most important stuff pretty quickly.

WHO can I bring with me?

You might be worried that you're not in the best position to go to a consultation, remember to ask all your questions, and store the information you receive away for future use. You really want someone else to be there, to help you, to ask the questions that wouldn't occur to you, and to hear what is said and help talk you through your options later on. You need moral support; you need a shoulder to lean on.

You need your mom.

Or your dad. Or your friend, sister, aunt, uncle, cousin, neighbor, or coworker. There are a million different places you might find the support that you need to get through that first consultation with a divorce lawyer, and there's no 'wrong' person.

Well, there is ONE wrong person. You can't bring your soon to be ex spouse.

A family law attorney can't represent both parties in a divorce action.

In some areas of the law – estate planning springs to mind – an attorney can represent both a husband and a wife, because their interests are aligned. They have a view for how to divide their assets, and they're going in together to accomplish it.

In family law, though, that's not the case. Though you're still married, you have separate interests – so you can't share the same lawyer. A lawyer has an ethical obligation to zealously represent her client's interests, and a family law attorney can't zealously represent both a husband and a wife. What if the wife needs spousal support and the husband doesn't want to pay it? Zealously representing someone doesn't mean meeting in the middle – it means representing your client's perspective, and your client's alone. It's an ethical conflict. No – you can't waive it.

You want someone to help you meet in the middle? You might be thinking more of a mediator. A mediator can work with both a husband and a wife, but definitely make sure you read up on the advantages and disadvantages of mediation before you sign up.

So, all of that to say: you can bring someone if you like, but that someone should not be your spouse.

Can I bring someone other than my spouse to my initial consultation for divorce?

Yes! Although there are some caveats, you can bring someone with you to your initial consultation for divorce.

Caveat #1: If you bring someone to your initial consultation, technically you're waiving your right of confidentiality.

Technically, having anyone else with you and your attorney while you have a privileged conversation (yes, this counts as 'privileged'), you waive confidentiality. You don't just waive it with respect to the three people in the room, though; you waive it globally.

If your third person is circumspect, it really shouldn't be a problem – after all, it's not like an attorney is going to run around blabbing about your case just because there was a third party in the room. But there are no rules binding your person to confidentiality, or anything stopping him or her from sharing the confidences that were shared in the room.

It's not always a problem, but occasionally it can be. Even though they usually are well meaning, I've heard of this third party intervening to try to save the marriage – with sometimes disastrous consequences for the people involved. If you can't trust the person that you're bringing into the room to be absolutely silent about their participation, then maybe you should re-think who you're bringing – if anyone at all.

Caveat #2: The topics discussed can be sensitive, so don't bring someone you can't be honest around to your initial consultation. Alternatively, if you want someone there but don't feel you can have the full conversation with them around, you could ask them to leave (or have the attorney do so).

Family law is one of the most human areas of law. We talk a lot about sex, religion, parenting, finances, and other hot-button issues that might be difficult for you to discuss in front of someone else.

If you aren't able to share, for example, that you have credit card debt and pay day loans in front of your dad, maybe you should leave him at home. If you can't admit that you and your husband were swingers, or discuss adultery (yours or his), or have an honest conversation about real sexual issues in front of your mom, maybe she's not the best person to bring.

An attorney can't be effective without accurate information, so make sure that you bring someone you can be honest around, and around whom you don't have to censor the information you share. If you can't be honest, you may be better off coming alone.

Caveat #3: Remember that this experience needs to be about you, not them.

You're not paying for a consultation so that your person can tell the attorney about your marriage, about their marriage, or their issues with your husband, or your divorce. If they can't be a (mostly) silent and totally sympathetic helper, then they're really not a great fit.

We don't need histrionics from someone else, or to deal with someone else's issues processing what you're going through. You need someone who can be there for you, so that no matter how you feel about it or how you respond to being in that consultation, you get the consultation you paid to have.

We're used to tears. We're used to anger, to frustration, to incredulity. We deal with substance abuse, mental health, domestic violence, and more – but we need to help our current and former clients, and not have extra to deal with from the people who our prospective clients bring along. It distracts us from focusing on who is most important: you.

You may love how your sister is a spitfire, but, in this application, she's your support person only. If she can't occupy the role you need her to occupy, it's better to kick her out.

Caveat #4: Your new romantic love interest is not the right choice, either.

Technically, you could bring a boyfriend – but it's not smart. And, anyway, it's not really appropriate.

Again, you're going to need to be completely honest in that appointment, and you don't want any distractions from the issues you need to handle.

It may be difficult to say what you need to say with your new flame in the room. You may be surprised by the questions the attorneys ask. You may not want your ex to have that level of detailed oversight into the process you're going through, your finances, or other issues. Even if your new boyfriend is paying for your consultation – or even your divorce – that does not justify giving him a seat at the table. If he's insisting on it, that's a red flag.

My advice? Handle your business. Then see your boyfriend.

It's also a concern from an adultery and/or spousal support perspective, so you should be aware. Keep in mind, too, that adultery is a criminal offense in Virginia as well. Even if you're 'talking' to someone, you shouldn't let it get beyond that point. Ideally, you'll wait until your divorce is finalized, but, at the very least, you should wait until you have a separation agreement signed.

Don't bring your boyfriend. Find someone else.

It's fine to bring someone along, if they're helping you. Dealing with a separation and divorce is hard under the best circumstances, and it's worse if you feel alienated, overwhelmed, and alone. If you have the right person in your life to help support you through the process, by all means, bring them.

The Attorney

Now, it's time to meet the attorney. In an initial consultation, it's pretty common for the prospective client (that's you!) to do most of the talking. Your attorney will want to hear, in your words, what's happening and what your goals are for the process.

As much as you want to get it all out, don't forget that you're also interviewing the attorney! Pay close attention to her. Is she taking notes? Listening to you? Addressing your questions? Does she 'get' it? Is she kind? Empathetic? Bored? Does she look at her phone? Is she willing to discuss several different scenarios with you? Does she have creative solutions to the problems you identify? Is she approachable? Can you be honest with her? (Are you being honest right now?) Do you feel like she's judgmental of you? Do you like her?

We want to do business with people we like. It's just human nature. And, ideally, you'll at least sort of like your divorce lawyer. It's not that we're here to win popularity contests but working with someone you like – and someone who understands where you're coming from and can hear even the messier parts of your case without judgment – will help make it a little easier. It's definitely not going to be easier if you can't be honest, and it's potentially disastrous.

Make no mistake, though: just because you like the attorney, or feel that she's empathetic, doesn't necessarily mean that she'll only give you advice that you want to hear. That's one of the hardest things in family law. There are many types of advice we have to give to our clients to put them in the best position possible that they aren't particularly thrilled to hear. Still, it's an important part of doing a good job.

When you get advice you don't want to hear

Being a family lawyer who represents women only – believe it or not – is not all sunshine and rainbows and fighting against narcissistic or abusive husbands. (Though there is a lot of that!)

I know. You're shocked. Sometimes, it's really, really hard. And one of the times when it's the hardest is when you have to give advice to your client that you know she's not going to want to hear.

"Now is not the time to be dating."

"Maybe you can't really afford to keep the house."

"You have to answer the discovery."

"You likely won't receive as much spousal support as you want for as long as you want."

"He's going to get at least some parenting time; in fact, he may get 50/50."

I gave some examples, just to put you in the right head space, but not to suggest that what I've come up with here is a complete and exhaustive list of the kind of advice that we could give that our clients would be less than happy to receive.

I'm a recovering people pleaser, so it is very hard for me to face truths that I know other people won't like – especially when their behavior is contributing to the problem and I have to explicitly point it out. But, like I said, I'm working on it. And, professionally, it really doesn't matter how I feel personally or whether something makes me uncomfortable. I am ethically required to represent my clients zealously, and that means that I have to be strong and deliver the bad news.

Yes, sometimes my clients get mad. Yes, sometimes they tell me that I'm working for "the other side". Yes, sometimes they ignore me. Yes, sometimes they lie to me.

There are four basic reactions to receiving less-than-favorable advice, in my experience:

1. Anger

2. Accusation

3. Ignoring

4. Lying

For each of those four reactions, I've written a response. Though I've written here from my own perspective, and with respect to my personal experiences, I think they're universally applicable. Keep in mind that, whether you meet with someone from our firm or somewhere else, the same basic facts are true: an attorney might give you advice that you don't like.

How you (and your prospective attorney) deal with differences of opinion will tell you a lot about what your working relationship will look like if you decide to hire that lawyer to represent you.

Anger

You are absolutely entitled to be angry. You're entitled to all your feelings. And, if I may be so bold, I think I'd posit that a lot of your anger is coming from a place of fear of the unknown. Of course, it may just be legitimate, garden variety anger, too – which is also fine.

I hate when clients are angry with me. I hate when anybody is angry with me. (Like I said – recovering people pleaser.) But I would also say, gently, of course, that your anger is misplaced. I'm not here to hurt you, or to keep you from having fun, or to do a bad job at being your lawyer. I don't want to hurt anyone, I like fun as much as the next person, and it is absolutely always my job to advocate as well for my clients as I can. But I also have to manage expectations, keep things reasonable, and, ideally, keep things moving.

Feel angry. Be angry. And, by all means, ask questions about my advice if you don't understand. Get a second opinion if you don't find that advice convincing, and you want to know whether someone else would give the same advice.

But, respectfully, I'd also suggest that the best thing for you to do – aside from asking questions or getting that second opinion (which, I assure you, will not offend me in the least) – is to try to deal with the anger itself. Talk to someone, preferably a therapist. What you're going through is a big deal, and you'd be inhuman not to be feeling really big, scary, overwhelming feelings about it. But deal with it in a healthy, productive way so that you're in the best possible position in your divorce. Don't let fear or trauma impact your judgment and hurt your case.

Accusation

"It's like you're my HUSBAND'S lawyer!"

"Are you just friends with my husband's lawyer?"

"Are you even representing MY best interests?"

I get it – you're upset. And you don't trust the advice, for one reason or another. That's totally fair. Divorce and custody cases are, in large part, out of your wheelhouse. And, in some cases, the advice runs counter to your instincts. You don't know me that well. And you're expected to just blindly trust me?

I mean, sure, it's easy to trust someone when they're not giving you bad news. In our initial consultation, you thought I was great! But now I'm giving you advice that (1) you don't like, and (2) doesn't feel right. It feels so wrong! And who am I, anyway?

I think it's a good idea to ask questions, if you don't understand, and to get a second opinion if you still don't trust the advice.

I can assure you, though, that I am not working for your husband. I've never represented men, and I certainly don't intend to start with your husband. Not only that, but I have an ethical obligation to represent YOU. I don't want to lose my law license.

I do, however, have a healthy sense of what happens in these types of cases. I don't pretend to have all the answers, but I do know a thing or two.

If you're feeling overwhelmed or fearful, it's probably a good idea to talk to a therapist or counselor about it. You're under a ton of pressure, and there's no question that these are really difficult circumstances.

If you still don't trust me – or whoever you're working with – maybe it just isn't going to work out. It's difficult to maintain an attorney/client relationship when the client is so doubtful about the advice, so here I'd also really push the whole second opinion thing, with the encouragement that, maybe, you really should just hire someone else.

Ignoring Advice

We typically give advice in our appointments. We're not in there with you in your day to day as you go about your life, actually following the advice you were given (or not).

So, some people decide that, as good as the advice might be, it's just not for them. They don't follow it.

It's your life. You're free to not follow the advice. But I definitely don't give advice for my health; the only reason I give advice (especially advice that my clients already don't want to hear) is to look out for them and help them avoid certain consequences. You aren't contractually required to follow advice, though. You're an adult, and you're free to do what you want.

But... there may be consequences. And you should be prepared for that. Maybe, even, you should ask, beforehand, what the consequences might be if you were to take a different course of action. (After all, this isn't a dictatorship!) If, for example, you're tempted to relocate with the child in violation of a custody order, talk to your attorney first. Maybe hearing the potential consequences of that action might cause you to change your mind. Always better to have an in-depth discussion ahead of time than to ignore advice and find out later that you'll live to regret it. Maybe you can live with the consequences. Maybe you can't. But definitely smart to talk about it ahead of time.

Keep in mind, too, that we aren't emotionally invested in the advice we're giving. To us, it's just a matter of best practice. It's not going to be offensive to us if you question that advice, especially if it seems wrong to you. It isn't a question of our personal opinion; it's just the law and our experience. If it doesn't make sense, ask questions! If it still doesn't make sense, ask a few more! A good attorney – an attorney worth hiring – is not going to get upset because you don't understand or want to make sense of something that is new to you. A lot of the advice we give isn't intuitive, so if you're confused, you're not alone. A good attorney will be happy to work through that with you.

And, above all, don't lie about having followed the advice, which leads me to number 4.

Lying

It's tempting to lie to save face, especially when you got (and discarded) perfectly good advice. From the perspective of your attorney, though, it's quite difficult to do a good job representing someone without having full access to all the facts.

It's quite easy to get tripped up in court, or wind up looking stupid, without a firm grasp of what's going on. And why on earth would you pay an attorney thousands of dollars to (1) not follow their advice, and (2) lie to them about it?

Going to court is difficult enough; going into court with an attorney who doesn't know all of the facts is terrifying. Don't do this. If you're going to not follow advice, at least be up front about it. An attorney who knows the truth – however less-than-desirable the truth might be – is infinitely better prepared than an attorney who has no idea what's actually going on. Don't do this.

Worst case scenario: you wind up with a result that you hate, and an attorney who withdraws from your case because of the untenable position you put her in.

At the end of the day, it's always up to you whether you follow advice that you're given – and, ultimately, you're the one who will deal with the consequences, if any. To best represent you, though, your attorney needs you to be up front and honest. Ideally, you'd have an open, realistic conversation about the options available to you, and the advantages and disadvantages of each course of action.

You hired an attorney, or at least sought the advice of an attorney, for a reason. It is entirely possible that now, or at some point in the future, you'll get advice that you don't like. My advice to you, in that situation, is (1) to deal effectively with any underlying issues, like trauma or fear, in therapy, so that you can make the best decisions possible, and (2) have a real, open, honest conversation with your lawyer about the advice, alternatives, and consequences.

Ultimately, if you're just in a stalemate, you should consider either getting a second opinion, or hiring someone else who is more in line with your views. Once the strength of the attorney/client relationship is undermined, it's difficult to recover. That's not a position you want to find yourself in, and, as the attorney, it's definitely not a situation I'd like to be in.

To make a long story short, I would suggest that it is possible both to get advice that you don't want to hear and be convinced that the attorney with whom you've met is the right person to represent you.

What questions should I be asking the attorney?

To tell you the truth, most of the time I don't get the third degree in my consults. Most people don't have a lot of questions to ask me about myself. They want to talk about their specific situation, and we spend most of our hour together talking about that.

But if there ARE questions you want answered – about your situation or the attorney's background – you should feel comfortable asking. Not sure what to ask? Here's a list you can use as a guide:

1. How long have you been practicing law?

When it comes to attorneys, experience definitely counts. Keep in mind that it usually takes years of handling cases and negotiating with opposing counsel before an attorney starts to learn and fully understand the full scope of family law strategies and tactics. By this time, the attorney has usually handled a lot of cases and has had exposure to many of the different issues and concerns that clients are facing in their divorce and child custody battles as well as the legal issues and strategies employed by the other side.

At the same time, you should also keep in mind that a younger attorney frequently costs significantly less per hour, even at a larger firm. Since you are preparing to go through a divorce and divide almost all of your assets in half, money is obviously a major concern for you. Oftentimes a younger attorney can be exactly what you're looking for. When an attorney is new, he or she is full of enthusiasm and dedication to your case and will often spend far, far more hours preparing than someone with more experience might. When deciding to use a less experienced but conceivably less expensive family law attorney, make sure they are part of a firm that practices family law exclusively.

2. Do you handle family law cases exclusively?

There are many attorneys who represent family law clients in addition to other practice areas, like personal injury and criminal law. You should work with an attorney whose practice is devoted 100% to family law.

Family law is an area of the law that is constantly evolving.

An exclusive family law practitioner will be able to keep current on changes in family law, which will be beneficial to you. A family lawyer will typically subscribe to various legal publications in his or her field of practice that address issues that are relevant to the practice of family law.

A lawyer who practices family law exclusively also devotes time to perfecting and mastering the unique courtroom skills necessary in custody and divorce cases. Although very few divorces make it through to trial, there are a number of different phases during the process in which your attorney may be required to present your case orally before the court. In a temporary support hearing, called "pendente lite" in Virginia, the lawyer has to present evidence and possibly question witnesses.

Divorces and child custody cases also require the lawyer to file motions on occasion—and that will also result in your lawyer having to go to court. When you get to court, you need to be assured that your lawyer will be confident when he or she is presenting your case.

3. Do you have an office policy regarding returning phone calls or emails?

Communication between attorney and client is key in any divorce action. A lawyer should be reachable by phone and email. Unfortunately, many clients' main complaints against their divorce lawyers are that lawyers fail to respond in a timely manner to their calls, emails, and other communications. Ask any lawyer you consider retaining whether there is an office policy regarding the prompt return of phone calls and emails. If the lawyer hesitates, there is most likely no such policy, and you will be frustrated to no end in trying to get in touch with him or her.

4. Who is your paralegal, what is her hourly rate, and what will she do on my case?

Family law attorneys usually work very closely with highly skilled paralegals. While each attorney/paralegal relationship is different, understanding what to expect can be really helpful. In many cases, the paralegal will be your primary point of contact – which is a good thing, considering a paralegal's hourly rate is much, much less than an attorney's.

Working closely with a paralegal can be a great way to save money on your case. To the extent that a paralegal can do some of the heavy lifting, it can save you a lot of money – while compromising none of the quality – on your case.

5. Have you handled many other cases like mine?

Though I would urge you to be cautious in asking this question – because no two cases are ever exactly alike – you're well within your rights to ask! Some types of cases do require an expert hand, like parental alienation or abuse, and you'll want to hear from your attorney that she is comfortable with the subject matter at hand.

6. What can I expect when I become a client?

In addition to legal services, are there any other services the law firm offers to its clients? A good lawyer is a great thing to have in your corner, but dealing with a divorce and/or custody case requires a more holistic approach. Good legal representation is a big piece of the puzzle, but so, too, is dealing with your mental and emotional health. It helps to work with a therapist through the divorce process, but it's even more helpful when your therapist or divorce coach are on the same page, so that your representation can proceed flawlessly.

Does the firm have resources to make sure that you understand what is happening and can make informed decisions in your case – or will you be relying on asking questions to attorneys or paralegals who'll bill you for their time?

Is there a sense of community? Divorce and custody cases can be a lonely time for many women. Just because you have a friend who is divorced doesn't necessarily mean that she'll be able to provide the kind of support that you need. You also probably don't have time, energy, or the extra money necessary to go out and meet people, either. It's helpful if your law firm sponsors events that can help you create a broader support network.

7. Are you often in court?

This might be a question you're expecting, but I suggest that you really listen to what the lawyer has to say. A lot of women will ask for recommendations – in fact, I see it all the time on social media – for a lawyer who is a "shark" or a "pit bull". While I can understand that sentiment behind it, because you're really reacting to feeling scared or powerless against something that feels much bigger than you, I often don't think that's the way to go.

"Oh, yes, I'm in court ALL the time," might not actually be the response you want to hear.

Attorneys who are sharks or pit bulls – or, at least, the ones in our community who develop that reputation – often get it because they behave in an overly aggressive and antagonistic way. The client may feel defended, but the end result often ends up taking longer, costing more, hurting everyone's mental health and, ultimately, not achieving the best results possible.

Really listen to your lawyer about her plan for your case. Consider how she'll move it forward. The best lawyers are not litigation happy; they encourage reasonable settlements and help clients develop skills that they can use to develop cooperative coparenting methods later on. Keep in mind that in divorce and custody cases there are two goals: (1) is to resolve the specific issue today, and (2) is to keep you out of court in the future. A good attorney can balance both, so that you are protected but also in a position to get the best possible result.

Listen to your attorney's answer, and pay attention to any subtext beneath the answer. Ask follow up questions if necessary.

It's a good idea to have consultations with more than one lawyer and compare their answers, how they handle your questions, and their plans for how to move your case forward. Use the attorney/firm evaluation form on the next page to keep track of your thoughts as you meet with each one.

Attorney / Firm Evaluation Form

This form is designed to assist you in evaluating the qualifications of the attorneys of law firms you are considering to help handle your case. <u>Make multiple copies of this form and fill it out after meeting with each attorney you are considering.</u>

Name of Firm: _____

Name of Attorney/Paralegal: _____

Location: _____

Phone/Email: _____

Website: _____

Cost of Consultation/Duration: _____

Retainer Fee Quoted: _____

Comments: _____

_____

_____

_____

_____

_____

_____

Years of Experience	0 – 5	5-10	10 – 15	15+
Family Law Experience	None	Some	Mostly	Only
Understanding of My Case	Not at All	Somewhat Misunderstood	Mostly Understood	Completely Understood
Has Attorney Successfully Handled Cases Like Mine?		None	Some	Lots
Website Content Quality	Bad, Poorly Made	Decent, Poorly Made	Decent Info	Abundant, Quality Info
Published	None	Few	Many	Lots
Articles	None	A Few	Many	Lots
Quality of Books, Articles, Instructional Videos, etc.	Bad, Poorly Made	Decent, Poorly Made	Decent, Well Made	Outstanding Quality
Excellent Client Review	No References Available	Some References	Mixed Reviews	Many Satisfied Clients
Attorney Listens to My Needs and Wishes	Talks Over Me	Practically Ignores Me	Decent Listener	Very Good Listener
Staff is Courteous and Responsive	Rude and Discourteous	Practically Ignores Me	Polite and Somewhat Responsive	Warm, Friendly, and Helpful
Law Firm / Attorney is Involved in the Local Community	Not Involved at All	Rarely Involved	Sometimes Involved	Very Involved

*Why would I want to **hire a divorce lawyer**, anyway?*

Additional Comments:

_____

_____

_____

_____

_____

_____

_____

_____

_____

_____

_____

_____

_____

_____

_____

_____

_____

_____

Conclusion

Divorce can be a scary process, but having an attorney on your side to help explain your rights and entitlements, help you understand the advantages and disadvantages of any course of action, and even help encourage you – when necessary – to advocate for yourself is one of the best ways to make sure that you get what you need through the process.

If you still need more information, we can help.

Consider attending our Monthly Divorce Seminars

For the past 30+ years, we've offered monthly divorce seminars to help Virginia women learn about the divorce process. The seminars are offered virtually on Zoom on the Second Saturday at 8:30am, the Third Tuesday at 6:30pm, and the Third Thursday at 12:00pm. Each seminar is taught by one of our licensed and experienced Virginia divorce and custody attorneys and features an opportunity to ask your questions directly to the presenting attorney and get your answers in real time.

The cost to attend is just $39.99, and you can register online at https://hoflaw.com/divorceseminar.

At our divorce seminars, we'll cover topics such as:

- Grounds for divorce
- How to be legally separated in Virginia (and why it matters)
- The difference between fault, no fault, contested, and uncontested divorce
- Why you might choose to file a contested divorce
- What alternative dispute resolutions (ADR) are available to you, including do it yourself, mediation, and collaborative divorce
- What a separation agreement is (and why you might want one)
- What an uncontested divorce hearing looks and feels like
- How property is divided in Virginia, including real estate and retirement
- How spousal support is calculated
- How custody and visitation are determined
- And more!

Check out Custody Bootcamp for Moms

Custody Bootcamp for Moms is an intense, all day custody seminar designed to help Virginia women learn what it takes to handle a custody and visitation case in the Virginia courts – with or without an attorney.

The seminar is offered live on Zoom, starts at 9am, and runs until about 3pm – or until the last woman's last question is answered. One of our experienced custody attorneys will present the seminar, but you'll get to see all of our attorneys at different points via different video presentations on a variety of topics.

At Custody Bootcamp for Moms, you'll learn:

- How custody and visitation decisions are made
- All about the ten best interests of the child factors (that the judge HAS to consider in making her decision)
- How to work with Guardians ad litem (and what they do)
- How to question and cross examine witnesses
- When to sit and stand and how to address the judge
- How to organize a trial notebook
- How to make opening and closing arguments
- How to deal with "special issues" in custody and visitation cases, like relocation and parental alienation
- And more!

These seminars are intense, so we only offer them quarterly – usually on the fourth Saturday of the month in January, April, July, and October. The cost to attend is $297, which is less than the cost of an hour with a moderately priced local attorney. Just like our monthly divorce seminars, you'll get a chance to ask all of your questions to our live attorney during the seminar.

You can register online at: https://custodyseminar.com.

Attend a Girl's Night Out Event

Divorce can be socially isolating. Whether you feel that your friends don't understand, that you lost your friends in the divorce, or even that, between marriage and motherhood, you just don't have any friends anymore, we're here to help.

Attend one of our Girl's Night Out events! They're free – and just a casual opportunity for similarly situated women (though no divorce or custody case is required, if you want to bring a friend along) to network and hang out. We've known several women to create lifelong friendships in this group and keep coming back even years and years later.

For more information on the next event or to register to attend, visit us online: https://hoflaw.com/gno.

Please note that registration is not strictly required – we're 'come as you are' people – but it does help us for planning purposes. Don't skip the event because you haven't registered, but register if you can. Bring a friend, too, if you like (there's space to do this on the form when you register yourself) – the more the merrier!

Apply for the Kristen D. Hofheimer Memorial Scholarship

Each year, we run an annual scholarship competition in honor of former firm owner (and daughter of firm founder, Charlie Hofheimer), Kristen D. Hofheimer.

Kristen passed away in 2019 after a struggle with breast cancer. We wanted to do something to honor her memory and legacy, and also to help support our clients. We figured that the perfect symbiosis between who Kristen was and what we wanted for our clients would begin and end with education – something that was incredibly important to Kristen.

Since 2019, we've given two $1,000 scholarships to two deserving Virginia women who are following a nontraditional path. For more information or to find out about our next scholarship opportunity – as well as our past winners – visit our website: https://hoflaw.com/register/kristen-d-hofheimer-scholarship/

If you're going back to school, we want to hear about it – and cheer you on every step of the way!

Divorce isn't one monolithic moment; it's a process.

From the time that you and your soon-to-be ex decide to separate, until your final decree of divorce is entered, and for years afterwards, you'll be navigating the divorce process. In the best cases, it's a holistic process that takes the particular woman in question and transforms her into the best possible version of herself.

Though effective legal advocacy is an important part of that, so too is education, forging friendships, and opportunity. We like to think that we have created our various programs – seminars, the scholarship, and our Girl's Night Out events – as a nod to all of the different parts of our current, former, and prospective clients that need to be nurtured, developed, and honed. The goal is to see you thrive through your divorce, not just survive it.

You are certainly not obligated to become a client of our firm by virtue of having read this book, but we're happy to make room if you want a seat at our table. You can visit our website at hoflaw.com to schedule an appointment (or to register for a seminar, request a free book or report, or to get more information about an upcoming Girl's Night Out event).

You can also request permission to join our HoflawVIPs group on Facebook. You'll have to fill in the security questions – we do our best to maintain the integrity of the group – but we'd be happy to have you. You can join here: https://www.facebook.com/groups/HofLawVIPs

Additionally, as a service to our clients, we offer a monthly support group. At the time of writing, this is not available to non-clients, but it's a service we believe in. Mental health is so important, especially at such a stressful and important time, and we wanted to make sure we were doing everything we could to meet all our clients where they are in their lives and to help make them better, happier, and healthier.

You're in the right place and you're asking the right questions. I sincerely hope this book is helpful to you and look forward to seeing you around at a seminar or Girl's Night Out event. We'd love to have you!

www.ingramcontent.com/pod-product-compliance
Lightning Source LLC
Chambersburg PA
CBHW062103270326
41931CB00013B/3187

* 9 7 9 8 2 1 8 6 2 0 1 2 7 *